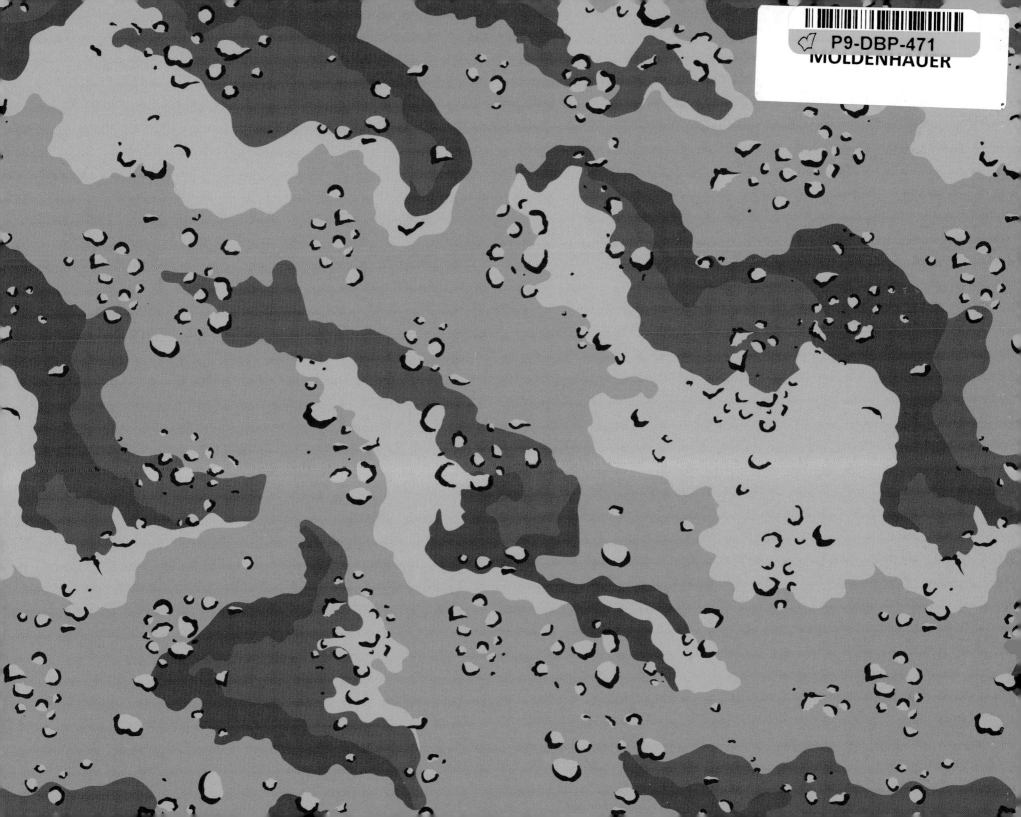

BOO BOO BEAR'S
MISSION

The True Story of a Teddy Bear's Adventures in Iraq

By Mary Linda Sather

Illustrated by children from military and civilian families

ISBN 10: 1-59298-283-2
ISBN 13: 978-1-59298-283-7

Library of Congress Catalog Number: 2009927043
Printed in the United States of America by Corporate Graphics Commercial, North Mankato, Minnesota
First Printing: 2009
Second Printing: 2010
Third Printing: 2013

16 15 14 13 12   7 6 5 4 3

Cover and interior design by Brenda Leavelle, Red Dirt Studios, Duluth, MN
Illustration photography by Brad Leavelle, Red Dirt Studios, Duluth, MN

BEAVER'S POND
PRESS

Beaver's Pond Press, Inc.
7104 Ohms Lane
Edina, MN 55439-2129
952.829.8818
www.BeaversPondPress.com

To order visit www.BeaversPondBooks.com or call 800.901.3480. Quantity discounts available.

About the Book

Boo Boo Bear's Mission tells the story of a beloved teddy bear on an important mission. Young Shea Leigh's dad has been deployed to Iraq with the Air National Guard. To help her dad feel less lonely while he is away from his family, Shea Leigh sends Boo Boo Bear to him in a care package. Half a world away from home, Boo Boo tours the base with Dad, embarks on a jet fighter flight, and fulfills an important mission—to carry a family's love until they can be together again.

This true story, related to the author by her son and granddaughter, brings comfort and reassurance to children whose families are experiencing the anxieties of deployment. The book includes a parent guide to assist families as they cope with the stress that often accompanies military family separations. Featuring charming illustrations drawn by children from military and civilian families, *Boo Boo Bear's Mission* offers a message of love and hope that can turn the difficulties of family separation into opportunities for growth.

A portion of the proceeds from the sale of this book will be donated to military family programs.

What Readers Are Saying

"I have tears in my eyes! This is absolutely the best kids' deployment book I've read. It identifies and validates the emotions of so many children in Air National Guard families. Helping our nation's smallest heroes understand the depth of their feelings isn't an easy task. Boo Boo Bear's Mission is a wonderful tool that can help give children words to express those feelings."

Jennifer Kuhlman, MN ANG 148th Fighter Wing
Family Programs Coordinator

"As a psychologist, who works with many hurting and grieving children, I know that anything that helps these children to open up and express what thoughts and feelings are inside them, is healing. This beautiful and heartfelt book will help them do that."

Catharine J. Larsen, M.A., Licensed Psychologist

"This wonderful story combines sensitive text with engaging children's illustrations. Mary Linda Sather provides the perfect blend of a heartwarming story and difficult subject matter. Boo Boo Bear's Mission serves as a springboard for discussion and caring. It would be a welcome addition in any classroom, library, or home."

Elizabeth Bartel, second-grade teacher and
2009 Nominee for Minnesota Teacher of the Year

"Boo Boo Bear's Mission is a sensitive, beautiful, and insightful story, honoring the depth of family connection and the resourcefulness of children and their families to thrive in love despite separation."

Sally Jo Blair, M.A., K-12 School Counselor and
author of a collection of resources for school counselors

"Boo Boo Bear's Mission is a wonderful and uplifting story that attests to a child's resourcefulness and a family's need for connection. Children separated from a parent may feel abandoned and bewildered and cannot always express their feelings. Sather provides personal understanding and practical ideas that allow such children openness and expression. Military families especially will find Boo Boo Bear's Mission an invaluable resource for the emotional tangles that confront them."

Judy Strong, writer, teacher, and author of *A Child's Grief: Surviving the Death of a Parent* and the award-winning *No Time to Grieve*

Dedicated to the military families

who have to say goodbye,

and to all families who are asked

to meet the challenges of separation.

Shea Leigh's dad was going away,

and she was feeling sad.

He was leaving for the war.

She was scared and she was mad.

Shea Leigh's dad was part of a team

that makes sure that the Falcons can fly.

He and the team made the jets safe

for their missions in the sky.

9

Shea Leigh begged her dad to stay at home,

then she wanted to sneak on his plane.

She had a horrible tummy ache,

but no one understood her pain.

Shea Leigh put on a big, brave smile.

Dad sadly shook his head.

Then she pouted, yelled, and cried

as she stomped off to her bed.

Nothing would take the ache away—

Shea Leigh lay on her bed forlorn.

She hugged Boo Boo Bear, her special friend,

who'd been her buddy since she was born.

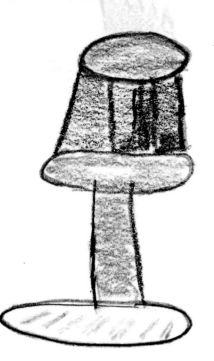

Boo Boo was now scrawny and scraggly with love.

He'd lost stuffing which had never been found.

But he comforted Shea Leigh with teddy-bear hugs

when her daddy wasn't around.

Too soon it was time for Dad to go,

with long hugs and sad goodbyes.

Boo Boo Bear showed his feelings, too,

as Shea Leigh wiped tears from his eyes.

Shea Leigh played basketball and worked hard in school.

Her friends helped her forget being sad.

Her mom did special things with her,

yet Shea Leigh still missed her dad.

Then one lonely day Mom said,

"Let's send some goodies to your dad.

I'll put in Swiss Rolls, muffins, and cookies.

Shea Leigh, what would you like to add?"

Shea Leigh said, "Daddy likes chocolate chip muffins!

He'll be glad for all the sweets.

But I think that he will need something else

besides goodies from home as treats."

25

"Dad might get lonesome—he might need a friend.

I'll send Boo Boo to sit on his knee.

Then every time he looks at my bear,

he'll think of home and me."

When Boo Boo arrived at the base, Dad grinned.

"Welcome to Balad, old bear!

I'm so very happy to see you again,

and proud that Shea Leigh wants to share."

Boo Boo was curious about Dad's job.

Where did the airmen sleep and dine?

So Dad gave Boo a tour of his sleeping pod,

the mess hall, and the jets' flight line.

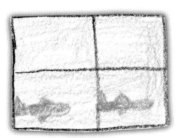

Boo Boo Bear liked the fast planes best—

they were shiny, sleek, and sublime.

What would it be like to go for a ride?

Boo Boo wondered about it all the time.

Every day, Boo Boo worked wherever Dad worked,

and each night he slept safe in Dad's pod.

With a flak vest and helmet on each of the bunks,

off to sleep the two airmen would nod.

Then came the day that Boo Bear had hoped for.

Dad said, "This bear needs to fly!

Now, no wild maneuvers—we don't want him sick.

Just whoosh him straight up in the sky!"

The pilot said, "Climb up in the cockpit with me

to share the mission lead."

The bear closed his eyes and held on tight

as the Falcon hit maximum speed.

The thrust of the jet pushed Boo back in his seat.

He stared as the ground whizzed by.

Then the roar of the engine quieted down

as the Falcon raced through the wide sky.

The crew chiefs and Dad all waited below

for Boo Boo to return to earth.

When the mission was done and the plane touched down,

they cheered for all they were worth.

43

That night, Dad called home to share the good news

that Boo Boo had done his part.

Shea Leigh knew that Boo Boo Bear would take care of her dad,

and she slept with a peaceful heart.

Boo Boo Bear was proud of his mission, too.

As a hero he was second to none.

Because he reminded the airmen of home,

each family, and every loved one.

After many adventures, Dad brought Boo Boo home.

Shea Leigh hugs them every day.

The three of them each served their country,

and are veterans in their own special way.

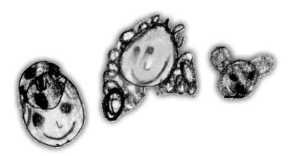

49

Thank you to all those who made the "Illustrators' Days" heartwarming and successful events!

☆ Megan Beatrez, age 14, page 21 | ☆ Mitchell Beatrez, age 13 | ☆ Audrey Beaudry, age 7 | ☆ Emily Beaudry, age 13, page 11 | ☆ Hannah Beaudry, age 11, page 23 | ☆ Breanna Beaulier, age 7 | ☆ Claire Beaulier, age 9, page 49 | Torie Carlson, age 14, page 15 | Bethany Crist, age 10, page 29 | ☆ Ryan Gressman, age 6 | ☆ Skylar Gunderson, age 9 | ☆ Zach Gunderson, age 7 | Bentley Hunter, age 9, page 9 | Anna Karas, age 10, page 31 | Catherine Karas, age 8 | Emily Klick, age 9, page 19 | Sierra Krupowski, age 14, page 17 | ☆ Jack Kuhlman, age 10 | Jesse Leavelle, age 5, page 43 | ☆ Michael McLean, age 6 | Sara McLean, age 11, page 7 | Tim McLean, age 15 | ☆ Cassandra Neumann, age 6 | ☆ Christine Neumann, age 10 | ☆ Gregg Nugent, age 11, page 41 | Camerron Reardon, age 11, page 45 | ☆ Cora Samuelson, age 5 | ☆ Leila Samuelson, age 7, page 27 | ☆ Levi Stauber, age 8, page 35 | ☆ Luke Stauber, age 7, page 33 | Dominick Stratioti, age 7, page 39 | Dalton Ulland, age 5 | Dayton Ulland, age 8, page 13 | ☆ Abbey Umali, age 9 | ☆ Denisha Walther, age 10, page 37 | Cole White, age 8, pages 25 & 47 | Connor White, age 7 | Keri Williams, age 13.

Principal Rudy Carlson, Stone Ridge Christian School, Duluth, MN | Dr. Jean Stevenson, University of Minnesota Duluth Department of Education and her students in the elementary education teacher education program: Andrea Burich | Melissa Cardenas | Jesse Frischmann | Katie Heltunen | Lana Peterson | Cassie Rice | Libby Schraw | Jessica Tewalt | Bobbi Wiinanen | ☆ Indicates child from a military family

How to Use This Book to Support Your Child

The following discussion topics and activity suggestions are intended to help you use *Boo Boo Bear's Mission* to support your child's emotional well-being as she or he deals with the stresses of a family member's military deployment. They have been developed from research-based psychological and educational practice. While much attention is devoted to the deployment period itself, be aware that stressors occur during the pre-deployment and reunion periods as well.

Some of these ideas may be appropriate to use while you read *Boo Boo Bear's Mission* with your child. Others will be helpful after you have finished the story or any time you sense that your child needs to talk. As a parent you know your child best. You are encouraged to modify what is offered and create new activities that will best meet the unique needs of your child and family.

In addition to informing close family and friends about the changes in your life, let teachers and other adults who have contact with your child (play groups, sports activities, clubs, church) know about your family member's deployment. Develop plans to keep communication open so everyone who is in your child's life can support him or her.

You may want to make the reading of *Boo Boo Bear's Mission* a family activity by inviting other family members to participate in discussions and activities. Children will learn from adults as well as other children that they are not alone in their feelings. They will receive emotional support, be encouraged to express and explore their feelings, and develop problem-solving skills for challenges they face when they and their families are separated from a loved one due to military deployment.

Let your child lead the way. Some children absorb information, process their feelings, and solve problems by themselves. Others need to process out loud with the guidance of another individual. Honor your child's style and always be aware of changes in behavior that could signal a need for help from an expert outside the family circle.

To Thrive During Times of Family Change Children Need:

- Physical safety and security: the reassurance that the adults in their lives are there to protect and care for them.

- Emotional support; a listening ear; acceptance of feelings without judgment; reassurance that their feelings and reactions are normal and that other family members may also feel the way they do.

- Reassurance that they have a safe emotional environment in which to express their feelings. Adults who talk about their feelings pave the way for children to talk about theirs.

- Developmentally appropriate answers to their questions.

- Opportunities to build confidence in their ability to be effective problem solvers, especially regarding ways of coping with the absence of a loved one.

- Familiar routines: predictability may lessen stress. If routines must change while a family member is deployed, help your child adjust by discussing what will be different and why.

- Acceptance from others of the diverse living arrangements that may occur due to separation from family members.

- Encouragement to find the positives in difficult situations. A parent or other family member who can talk about a sky that is partly sunny, rather than one that is partly cloudy, can serve as a powerful role model for a child.

- Resilience: the ability to effectively cope with and quickly recover from challenging experiences.

The three sections in this guide: **Feelings, Family Connections,** and **Healthy Coping Strategies** offer you specific information and ideas about how you can support your child as you enjoy *Boo Boo Bear's Mission* together.

Feelings

Talking about Feelings

It's reassuring to kids if a parent or caregiver can talk about what she or he feels and what coping skills she or he uses. Talking about feelings helps children expand their "feelings" vocabulary so they can express feelings more precisely and comfortably. It helps children make connections between feelings, thoughts, and actions, so they can understand themselves better. It gives parents or caregivers insight into what is going on in the child's mind so the adult is more able to assist the child.

Here are a few questions to start a conversation about feelings.

- How did Shea Leigh feel when she knew her dad was going away?
- How did you feel when you found out Mom/Dad/other loved one would be going away?
- What was the first thing you thought when you found out?
- How have your thoughts and feelings changed?

Feelings Activities

Use feeling words with your child in daily conversations to help build a feelings vocabulary. The level of sophistication will vary according to the age of the child.

1. Create a feelings dictionary by making a list of feelings words your child suggests and adding words of your own. Include a wide range of feelings, both positive and negative. Write each word on an index card, paper plate, a long piece of plain wrapping paper taped to a wall, or a home-made scrapbook with one page for each word. Add drawings of faces that express each feeling word. If drawing is not your talent, use magazine pictures instead. Encourage your child to decorate the dictionary with additional drawings or stickers.

2. Use your dictionary to play games.

    "Guess How I'm Feeling"

    First player chooses a facedown card or a paper plate and expresses that feeling using a facial expression and body language. Other players guess what feeling word is being expressed. First one to correctly identify the feeling gets the next turn. If you are using a strip of paper or a scrapbook as your dictionary, a player may secretly choose a word, then continue with the game as described.

    "Feel, Think, Do"

    First player selects a feeling word from the dictionary and says, "When I feel _____ (whatever the card says) I _____ (describes with words or acts out what he or she thinks and/or does when feeling that way). Create a way to decide who goes next. This activity may present opportunities to talk about alternative ways of dealing with feelings.

3. Make sock puppets that represent family members and use them to talk about and act out feelings.

4. Have a time during the day to gather as a family and talk about how the day has gone for each family member. You could use open-ended sentences such as the following to start the discussion.

Something good/nice that happened today was… and I thought/felt…

Something bad that happened today was… and I thought/felt…

The best thing that happened today was… and I thought/felt…

The worst thing that happened today was… and I thought/felt…

What I liked about today was…

What I didn't like about today was…

The responses you hear will let you know what is on your child's mind. With that information you will be able to guide further discussion to meet your child's needs.

Family Connections

Talking about Family Connections

When a family member is temporarily separated from the family, children need to be reassured that their loved one is still a part of the family. Talking about family connections keeps the family unit together in spirit. It makes the absent member's experience more real to the child and connects the child to that experience. It supports the absent family member by including her or him in ongoing activities at home.

Here are a few questions to start a conversation about family connections.

- What did Shea Leigh and her mom do to feel close to Dad while he was away?
- What else could she have done?
- What can we do to feel close to _____ while he or she is away?
- What will you like the best when _____ comes home?

Connecting Activities

Set aside a regular time, daily if possible, for discussion and activities that will help to strengthen the family unit during the deployment.

1. Use a journal, scrapbook, or envelope to keep a record of family activities, children's art work and school work, and photos to mail to your family member or to share when he or she returns.

2. Take photos or make videos or DVDs with your loved one before the deployment. Once your loved one has deployed, make a special event out of looking at the photos or DVDs and talking about your absent family member.

3. Before your loved one leaves, create a special evening or bedtime ritual that can be continued while she or he is away. Kiss your loved one's picture. Choose a favorite book to read, sing a favorite song, or recite a special prayer. For older children, the ritual could be listening to a shared favorite song, reading a shared favorite poem, or going for a run.

4. Before your loved one deploys, have a family discussion about things you love about that person, activities you enjoy doing with him or her, silly things that person has said, and so forth, and write each one on a small piece of paper. Put the pieces of paper in a container and during the deployment pick one out to talk or smile about anytime your child is especially missing the absent family member. You could also include the deploying person's special thoughts about family members and put them in a separate container for him or her to take along.

5. Help your child to write and send letters to your absent loved one. Letters written in a child's own handwriting or a picture drawn by your child can help both the child and the absent family member feel connected.

6. If possible, set up a predictable schedule to call your absent loved one and to send and receive email messages.

7. Send audio or video tapes to your loved one. Set up a way for your family member to record and send audio tapes to you. (Your local or regional military family network may be able to help you with this. See #5 in the website listings.)

8. Put a photo of your absent family member or the entire family in a plastic envelope for your child to carry in his or her pocket, backpack, notebook, or wallet.

9. Make and decorate a calendar to be used to record important events that occur while your family member is away. This can be shared upon his or her return. When the date of return is known, the calendar can also be used to count down the days.

10. If the deployment area is known, keep a clock set to that time and discuss with your child what your loved one is doing at different times of the day. Compare that activity with what the rest of the family is doing at home. Display a map of the area and research the land and people of that area with your child.

11. Use puppets to have make-believe conversations with your absent loved one.

Coping Strategies

Talking about Healthy Coping Strategies

Children develop many different kinds of behaviors in response to challenging life situations. Some behaviors are counterproductive; some are helpful. Healthy coping strategies are approaches that help children deal effectively with challenging life situations. To remain physically, psychologically, and emotionally well, a military child must be able to accept and adjust to a loved one's temporary absence during deployment. This requires that a child be able to productively manage feelings that are sometimes overwhelming. It also requires a child to develop behaviors that allow her or him to function successfully in a changed environment. When children are successful at managing emotions and behavior, they will be empowered to solve problems. With that success comes confidence. They will be better able to look forward to a time when the family is reunited and they will more readily believe in a positive future.

Here are a few questions to start a conversation about coping strategies.

· What did Shea Leigh do to help herself feel better while her dad was away?

· What can you do to help yourself feel better?

· What do you think would help you the most?

· What can we do together as a family to help us feel better?

Activities for Building Healthy Coping Strategies

Talk with your child when she or he is having a difficult time. It is vital to acknowledge feelings of sadness, loneliness, anxiety, confusion, anger, and so forth. Once your child's feelings have been acknowledged, she or he may be ready to engage in the activities suggested in this section. Redirecting your child to something positive and fun is often an effective way to build coping strategies.

1. Role playing may give your child an excellent opportunity to develop effective coping strategies. For example: if your child is being teased because a parent is absent from school functions due to deployment, you and your child can practice what he or she might say that will help ease the awkwardness of the situation. For younger children, role-playing with puppets is another option.

2. Participating in a school-based or military family network kids' group may help your child feel less alone, by introducing him or her to other children who are experiencing many of the same feelings.

3. Encourage older children to keep a journal to record feelings, events, and both successful and unsuccessful coping strategies they have tried. If your child wishes to share, you may have an opportunity to support and guide her or him through the problem solving process.

4. Keeping a list of ideas for family activities to do when your family member returns home can help children develop a positive and hopeful outlook. Be sure to solicit and include the absent member's ideas in your list.

Websites

These websites are excellent resources for providing assistance, information, and activities for your children and you as you deal with the pre-deployment, deployment, and reunion phases of military life.

Deployment Kids
www.deploymentkids.com

Includes free downloadable activities for kids.

Military Kids Connect
www.militarykidsconnect.org

Resources and activities for kids from 6–18 as well as teachers, parents, and caregivers.

Sesame Street Talk, Listen, Connect Initiative
www.sesamestreet.org/parents/topicsandactivities/toolkits/tlc

Video stories with the Muppets to help preschool children cope with the transitions and separations that often accompany military family life. Strategies, resources, and references for parents.

Military Families Near and Far: Expanded Resources for Military Families
www.militaryfamiliesnearandfar.org

Resources for elementary school-aged children and their parents that include printable activities.
(Developed by Sesame Street and The Electric Company)

The Military Child Education Coalition
www.militarychild.org

Includes publications, programs, and other helpful websites for military families with children of all ages.

The National Military Family Association
www.nmfa.org

Offers resources on topics of deployment, education, and family life.

Acknowledgments

Without the seasoned advice, generous contributions of time and talents, and loving encouragement of family, friends, community members, and skilled professionals, the book *Boo Boo Bear's Mission* would have remained just another poignant and private family story.

I offer my gratitude and thanks to the many people who made contributions to this project: Sally Jo Blair, Carl Freund, Ann Harrington, Voula Heffernan, Shelley Maas, Taylor Schmidt, Brenda Sederberg, and Judith Tollerud. In their various roles as loyal friend, project volunteer, reader and informal editor, idea generator, cheerleader, and therapist, they gave me the gift of constancy.

The Beaver's Pond Press staff, most particularly my production editor, Amy Cutler, and my editor, Kellie Hultgren, helped me cross the bridge between writer and published author. Thank you for your high level of professionalism, patience, suggestions, insights, and creativity.

The deployed members of the Minnesota Air National Guard 148th Fighter Wing have my deepest respect and thanks for their service to our country. Beyond the call of duty, their generous hearts cheered a lonely little girl when they embraced a scraggly teddy bear from halfway around the world.

Brad Leavelle's photographs reveal the beautiful intensity of children at work. His cover photo of the real Boo Boo Bear perfectly captures the spunky character of the bear who traveled so far on a mission of love.

Jennifer Kuhlman, the Family Programs Coordinator for Duluth's Air National Guard 148th Fighter Wing, was a whirlwind of ideas, skilled organization, and positive support for the entire project. Her belief in the importance of getting Boo Boo Bear's story out to kids and families helped to keep the project going.

Brenda Leavelle deepened the child illustrators' visions of *Boo Boo Bear's Mission* and made the book whole with her superb design work. Our relationship became a gift as she inspired me with her professionalism, creativity, and sense of humor.

Love and thanks to my family: husband Jim Howe, son Ron, daughter-in-law Karri, and granddaughters, April, Brittanie, and Shea Leigh Waterhouse, and my sister Kristin Pabst for their enthusiastic encouragement and steadfast belief in me.

Finally, it is with pride, admiration, and love that I salute Shea Leigh, my remarkable granddaughter. Her great love for her dad and her willingness to sacrifice something very precious to show that love brought *Boo Boo Bear's Mission* to life.

About the Author

Mary Linda Sather is the mother of a member of the Air National Guard, a grandmother, and a great-grandmother. As a parent and as a long-time educator, she has witnessed the stressful effects separation can have on families.

When her son called from his second deployment in Iraq to tell her that his youngest daughter, Shea Leigh, had sent her teddy bear to him to keep him company, Mary Linda was deeply touched. She knew that she wanted to turn that experience into a story with a reassuring, happy ending that could be shared with other military families.

Mary Linda lives with her husband, Jim, and a tuxedo cat named Keeda in Duluth, Minnesota, home of the Minnesota Air National Guard's distinguished 148th Fighter Wing. She enjoys spending time with family and friends, reading, yoga, traveling, and hiking.

Mary Linda has previously published travel articles in the *Michigan AAA* and *Boating* magazines. This is her first children's book.